P9-CFA-274

MAR 19

GRAMMAR'S SLAMMIN'
Find Your Function at
Conjunction
Junction

By: Pamela Hall
Illustrated by: Gary Currant

magic Wagon

visit us at www.abdopublishing.com

Published by Magic Wagon, a division of the ABDO Group, 8000 West 78th Street, Edina, Minnesota 55439. Copyright © 2009 by Abdo Consulting Group, Inc. International copyrights reserved in all countries. All rights reserved. No part of this book may be reproduced in any form without written permission from the publisher.

Looking Glass Library™ is a trademark and logo of Magic Wagon.

Printed in the United States.

Text by Pamela Hall
Illustrations by Gary Currant
Edited by Stephanie Hedlund and Rochelle Baltzer
Interior layout and design by Neil Klinepier
Cover design by Neil Klinepier

Library of Congress Cataloging-in-Publication Data
Hall, Pamela.
  Find your function at conjunction junction / by Pamela Hall ; illustrated by Gary Currant.
     p. cm. -- (Grammar's slammin')
  Includes bibliographical references.
  ISBN 978-1-60270-615-6
  1. English language--Conjunctions--Juvenile literature. I. Currant, Gary, ill. II. Title.
  PE1345.H35 2009
  428.2--dc22
                        2008036318

Ring-ding-jingle rang the doorbell as Babs Baxter tore into the conjunction store.

"Please help me!" pleaded Babs. "I'm beach-bound and I have kids running around. I can't get organized!"

Conjunction
Junction
"Sentences Fixed In A Jiff"

3

"What can I do for you?" asked Ben, the function finder at Conjunction Junction.

"We wanna swim!" shouted twins Drew and Sue.

"I just can't win!" Babs gasped. "Can you help me get these things put together?"

"You need a conjunction to string your items together into a sentence," Ben explained. "Then you'll have your hands free and be organized as can be."

"Conjunctions?" wondered Babs.

"Conjunctions put words and thoughts into phrases, sentences, and paragraphs," said Ben. "And, but, and or are the most common conjunctions. The word *and* can string together all your beach gear. Just say: *Pack up your towels, toys, and flippers.*"

"Thanks!" Babs called, as she grabbed the bags and breezed out. "We're back in business!" As she left, a guy named Ty slid in with a sign.

Ben

"The Stilton Hotel needs a better sign," said Ty. "People need to see that we offer more than the Blitz Hotel." He handed Ben brochures from both hotels.

Ben flipped through the brochures. "The Blitz charges extra for cable, high-speed Internet, and breakfast. We can use the conjunction *but* to show that the Stilton is the best deal."

Ben worked fast to find the conjunction with the best function. Soon the words were in place, and Ty left with a smile on his face.

You coul

the s

Soon, the doorbell *ring-ding-jingled* again.
"Please help me with my menu of the day!" Chef Jeff exclaimed. "Customers must know what comes with the main entrée."

Chef Jeff watched Ben blend words and conjunctions to make his menu.

nor

but

MENU

Each meal is a d

Isn't that ni

Salad

a

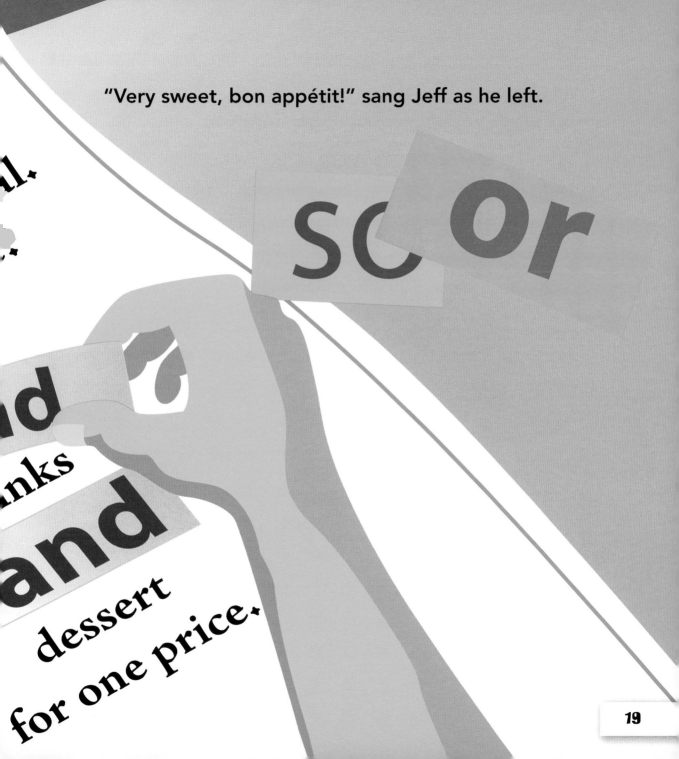

"Very sweet, bon appétit!" sang Jeff as he left.

SC or

nks

and

dessert

for one price.

Next, Ben hammered signs for a day care. Bonnie was relieved to have her slogan for all to see.

Bring Baby to w

drop him by

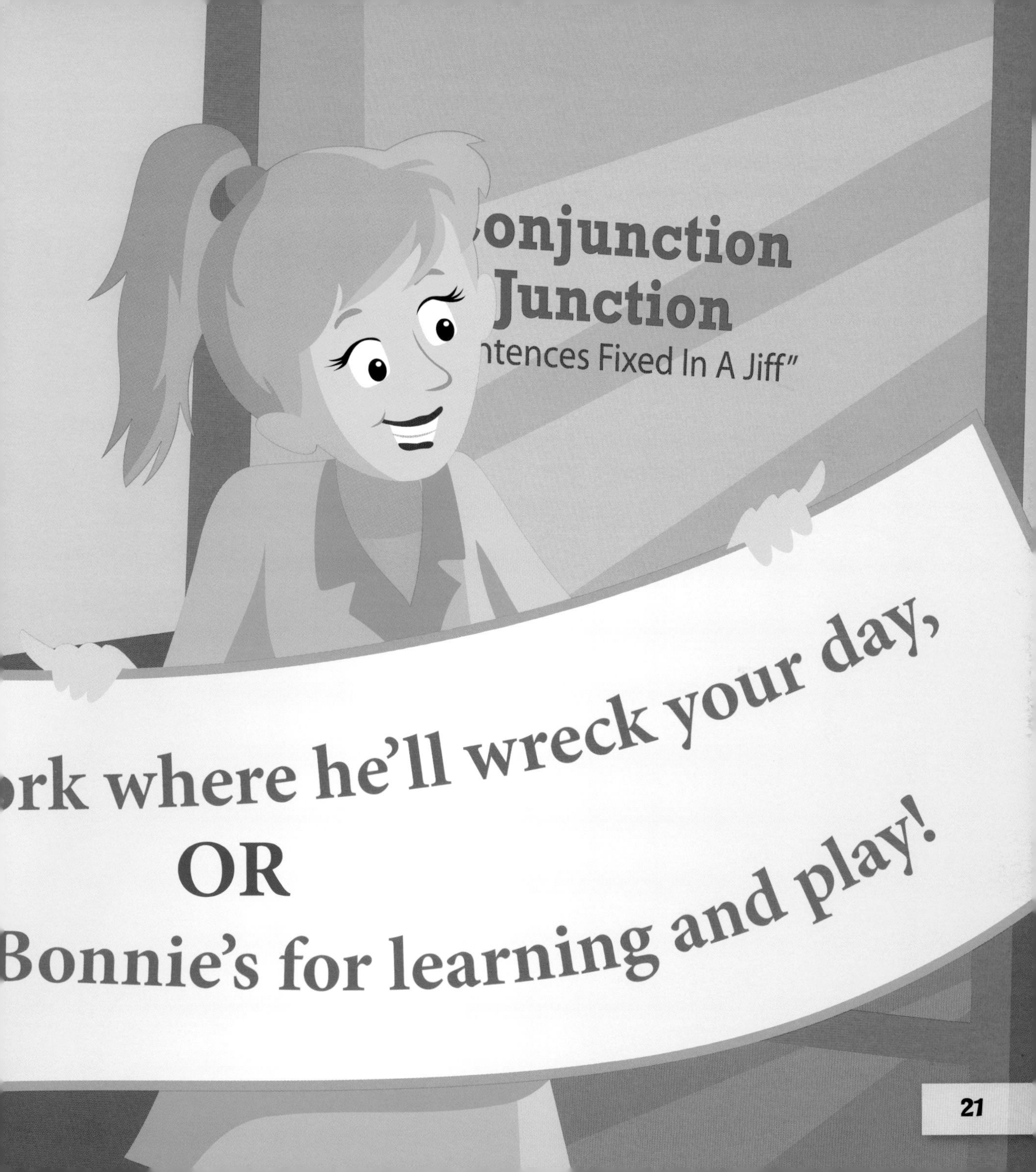
onjunction
Junction
ntences Fixed In A Jiff”
rk where he’ll wreck your day,
OR
Bonnie’s for learning and play!

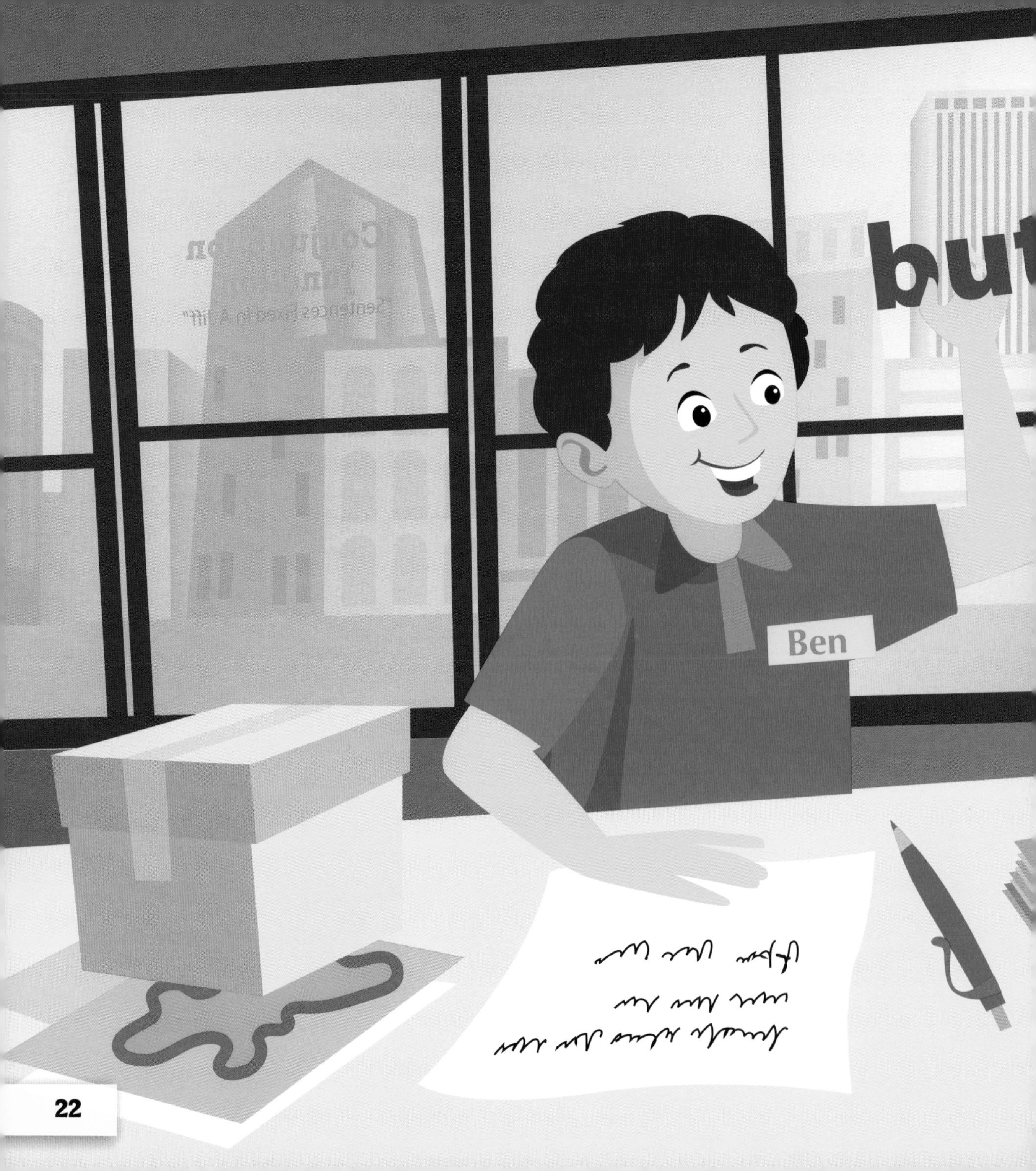
but
Ben

The rest of the day was busy for Ben. He reworked brochures and designed ads. He even drew up a team roster for a group of dads.

Chicken and dumplin's

Texas or Bust

Then, right at closing time, the doorbell *ring-ding-jingled* once more.

"I need a sign for my airline in the sky," said Kyle. "People must know it's fastest to fly."

Conjunction Junction

"Sentences Fixed In A Jiff"

"All you need are three conjunctions. Here you go," said Ben.

You can wast
BUT it's q
join us for a r

time with a drive,
icker to fly, so
e AND see the sky.

As Ben was closing up shop, he got a fax from his boss. He had to fill in the missing conjunctions to get his bonus. Can you think of the missing conjunctions to help Ben out?

You
café, a.

"I've rolled today's projects _____ signs to one
It will spell a surprise once you are done."

'You might drive a car, _____ a plane's the fast
track to fun. _____ grab your conjunctions for
week in the sun.

uld splash at the beach _____ check out a
quest of the Stilton, you'll have it your way.'"

More on the Function of Conjunctions

Conjunctions link together words and phrases into sentences. *And*, *but*, *or* and *so* are the most common conjunctions. There are seven conjunctions in all. They spell out this silly word:

F	A	N	B	O	Y	S
for	and	nor	but	or	yet	so

These smaller words hook thoughts and phrases into complete sentences.

FOR is a rather stuffy conjunction used to introduce the reason for the preceding clause. An example is, *Mom knew a headache was forming, **for** her children were still fighting.*

AND joins nouns together. Like, *You **and** your sister are going to the mall.*

NOR is usually used as a joiner in a negative statement. As in, *The kid was neither well-behaved **nor** quiet.*

BUT and **SO** join sentences together. For example, *We were going to, **but** she pinched me again, **so** I stayed home.*

OR joins verbs with verbs. As in, *Stop fighting **or** there will be trouble.*

YET can mean "in addition to," such as **Yet** *another argument*. It can also mean "still," as in **Yet** *more troublesome*. Finally, it can mean "eventually," such as *They may **yet** figure out how to get along.*

Always remember, when using a conjunction to join two sentences, use a comma before the conjunction.

*"We were going, **but** she hugged me again, **so** I had to hug her back."*

Next time you are fighting with your brother or sister, make sure you get that extra punch in with the proper use of conjunctions.

*...**or** I'm telling Mom on you, **and** she'll be mad! **So** you better mind your manners and your grammar.*

Web Sites

To learn more about grammar, visit ABDO Group online at www.abdopublishing.com. Web sites about grammar are featured on our Book Links page. These links are routinely monitored and updated to provide the most current information available.